THE 24 HOURS BLOGGING LESSONS:

How to work from home and make money from your spare time with nothing more than computer network

Philip   Knoll

ISBN-13: **978-1985896666**

DEDICATION

To my parents, patty jean, James Knoll and my loving wife Diana , who is a constant source of encouragement, love and positive energy.

Table of Contents

FREE BONUS

P.S. AS a token of my appreciation, I have included a free gift for you no catch, no charge. simply click www.itechcrown.com

Chapter one

Introduction

1 Hour

welcome to most effective practical guide to the Bloggers. The times are allocated to this chapter is four hours and divided into the section that provides background information to help you understand the basics of blogging and shows you where can sources of valuable reference material that will help to achieve your goal. We also mention a number of different blog types, how to select your niche, and list of the many reasons why people like to blog.

Blog and Blogging

On August 23, 1999 Blogger was launch as one of the earliest dedicated blog-publishing tools. A blog shortened as the phrase "weblog" it is a well known as many things that consist of differences digital material such magazine, diary, newscast, collector's meeting place, a showcase for your art, information sharing, teaching hub, the place to learn almost anything you want it to be. A typical blog joint text, images, videos and links to relevant pages and media on the Web. At the same times, Blog readers can leave comments and communicate with the author. In fact, it is space for dialogue and interaction which is a popular part of a blog's success.

In the blogging terms, you would have heard the word

- ➢ Blog means an online journal.
- ➢ Blogger is the person who owns and contributes to a blog.
- ➢ Blogging is the act of creating content for the blog).

You can choose to be any one of the following:

- ➢ Blogger, blogging on a blog.

> Blog about a blogger blogging.

> Blogging blog about a blogger."

One of the most important aspects about blogging is that it has made on communication throughout the world better and simples. Blogs can report any news as it happens, hold mainstream media to higher standards, and provide a specific news and information to meet particular niche interests.

According to Darren Rows, one of the initial and best-known bloggers defines Blog like this:

A blog is a type of website that is usually arranged it contents in chronological order from the most recent 'post' (or entry) at the top of the main page to the older entries towards the bottom.

It has been believed that about 82% of US online consumers trust information and advice from the blog while a small business that get 126% more leads growth compared to that do not blog.

The types of blogs

The most popular types of blogs are many and more to be discovered. The context of this book will only be narrowed to few of them. There are community blogs, non-profit blogs, live-webcam blogs, live-gaming screen-cast blogs, device-type blogs, podcast blogs, various video blogs, and many, more others. Few of But most important, and you need to learn the difference between the blog and a static website.

We always recommend webbing newbie's and novice to start a blog, in order to learn the basics features of the online presence. But if you are looking to promote your business online maximally (or to start a new one) then it's better to learn how to make a website instead.

How to select blog type   2 hour

Personal blogs

Personal blogs always share thoughts, original art, poems, writing, or photography etc. Some Blogs sell custom crafts, art, or products. If you just want to make an account, show your DIY (do it yourself) skills, have fun or blog for therapy, a personal blog is perfect for your needs.

Business blogs

Business blogs are created in the name of the company, as a crucial component of marketing. They can function as a direct-sales tool and are exceptional for both messaging and two-way communication system as part of a company's public relations efforts. Blogs are effective and cost-efficient means for small organizations that need to publish information for their customers or their members.

Niche/topical blogs

Niche focus on a particular interest. They can be about different lifestyles on health, gardening, education, sports, fashion, and politics. Now choose your special field of interest and you can blog about it. If you're a collector of antiques, a true-mystery fan, and a travel addict or just love cooking, there may be a blog in your future. Niche blogs can easily attract loyal followers, which contributes to the fun of blogging.

Media-type blogs

Media-type blogs are defined by their multimedia contents. If you enjoy video blogging, then you're a vlogger. If you are getting your content from other websites, you have a linkblog. If you post a photos or art sketches on your blog, you're hosting a photoblog or art blog respectively.

Reverse blogs

The reverse blog is an exclusive but popular type of blog. In this type instead of the owner creating his content, the content is supplied by the public members. A reverse blog must have a team leader, who can assign a moderator to moderates posts, prevent unpleasant interactions, and promote slow topics flowing for greater interactivity.

WHY DO YOU WANT TO BE A BLOGGER?

Why do like to start a blog? Think about why are you starting a blog,and why people should be interested in following your blog. Dr.Jeff Bullas created a poll and asked thousands of people, "Why do you blog?.The answers differ, but top answers were,"Writing about the passion" and "To share thought with others".

Benefits of blogging

If you want to become a greater writer and thinker once you start blogging, you'll find yourself becoming a better writer, and thinker. Mastering content is a gradual process through creative thought. When you become immersed in creating great pieces of content for your blog, your writing, thinking and research skills improve by the days.

It can make you as an expert

Blogs are wonderful tools to assist people to establish themselves as experts in a field of their interest. We all have some kind of interest and expertise to share with others. If you're able to create great content on your blog and/or have a unique point of view on the topic, and then be assured that your future audience will recognize it and reward you for it.

Today, the internet web has different experts and different opinions for almost every topic you can think up. With a little of effort, you too can become an authority in the area of your interest. So be ready now and good luck.

Raise your self-confidence

The more involved you are the more you become with blogging, the more your creative juices will flow. That's one reason why blogging is so popular. As you gain more knowledge about your topic, the confidence you'll build in your followers and most importantly, in yourself. This entire can leads to increase your creativity. According to the one international journal, stated that 81 percent of Americans believe they have a book inside of them to share with the world. In essence, you will be able to write a book, piece by piece, on your blog. Keep an open mind and enjoy your new-found confidence in your own abilities.

Make friends and have fun

With constant practice and a little effort, you can easily build your base of blog fans and followers. As you become known as an expert in your niche, you can inspire, encourage, and help your followers make a difference in their own lives. I can assure you that along with your blogging journey, you will make a lot of new friends and connections throughout the world. If you like to travel, that means a lot of coaches are available for you to snooze on while winging your way around the globe.

You can make money from your blog

You can derive a financial gain from your blogging journey. You can place ads and receive affiliate commissions by promoting products of established online retailers. You can create and sell your own digital products and merchandise. We will discuss much of this in chapter 6.

How to select a perfect niche   3 hour

This time I am going to you offers an interesting approach for selecting the best niche for your success as a top blogger.

How select a niche for your new blog.

The best way to choose a niche is to pick one that appeals to you. If you want to attain the highest form of knowledge in the niche/topic of your choice, then pick the one you are passionate about and most interested in. Your desire for success, happiness, security, and recognition depend on that. By choosing your niche of interest and having your own point of view you'll be able to make and differentiate your blog from the competition. Remember that, the meaning of life is in attaining the highest form of knowledge, which is the idea of the good."

Come up with your topic

Following is a process that can increase your potential and helps you to determine which niche is best for you:

> ➤Make a general list of your interests or hobbies. Which topics fascinate you more? List them all, for instance: golf, fishing, and study, yoga, playing games or cooking.

➢ List life accomplishments you are proud of, such as musical talent, artistic talent, or sports achievements

➢ List difficulties you encounter in life and how you have overcome them, such as: losing a significant amount of weight,recovering from a financial setback or managing a chronic disease.

In the process of doing the above come up topic choice, you will get a better feeling for the topics that suitable for you. The ones that you are most passionate about are the best candidates for your niche.

Blog success justification

Whether you want to blog for reputation, income, fun, or connections, you'll have to research the niche you choose and make sure the topic is viable, reliable. The following blog success justification exercise will help you determine whether your blog has real potential. It will also help you to understand that, why most blogs fail, and ways to avoid it.

Niche size

Even if you believe you have a brilliant, radiant blog idea, you will likely struggle to succeed unless if you find a niche market that attracts enough people or one with low competition. Your niche should not be too small or too big.

The size of "golf" niche is, on average, more than 2.9 million monthly searches. This niche might be too big and too broad as a beginner blogger.

On the other hand, if you pursue a niche that is very narrow, such as plane "golf swing drills" (average 3,000 searches monthly), the volume of searches would be too small. The best way to drill down from "golf" would be "golf tips"(average 370,000 total monthly searches)or even deeper down "golf tips for beginners"(average 260,000 total monthly searches).

Verify the size of your niche

Make sure you check the top five keywords for your niche market. Look for at least 10 thousand monthly searches combined for the five keywords. You can use Google Keyword Planner or Kwfinder these two are free, while Market Samurai and WordTracker are paid version that helps you to check for the volume of searches and get keywords ideas. You want to be sure that, there is a large enough audience looking for the kind of information you will provide, but not so large that you will get lost in the crowd.

How to use the Google Keyword Planner tool

➤ This Google tool is used to get top keyword ideas and search volume:

➤ on the search bar Select the "Search for new keyword and group ideas" tab. Enter your main keyword (Examples in our "golf tips") and get ideas by looking at the list of suggested keywords.

➤ Select the top five keywords that fit the niche market you chose.

➢ Check the search volume for each keyword and sum them up together.

The following are the result of the search process to our five golf-tip keywords, yielded the following search results:

➢ "golf tips" 9,800

➢ "golf swing tips" 8,00

➢ "golf putting tips" 1,200

➢ "golf tips for beginners"   860

➢ "golf tips driving"   490

With these five keywords, we have over 20,000 average monthly searches. This niche market ("golf tips") has enough generated volume and would be a good choice for your blog.

Potential competition 4 hour

It's a good sign if you have the competitive site. It means others are talking about your niche and actively pursuing it. It's also very important to note that bloggers in your niche are not always your competition.

You can follow these competition review process:

> Can you find some blogs currently targeting your niche?

> Are there at least five trendy blogs focused on your topic?

> Do a Google search for"[niche] blog" or "best [niche] blogs."

> Don't lose interest if you see a large number of blogs in your niche.If they can do it, so go ahead.

> Go to Facebook and also do a search for your niche. Are there active any Facebook pages?Not all topics provide themselves to Facebook, but most do.

> Look for Facebook pages and see how many followers they have.Great niches will exhibit at least 2,000 fans.

> Are there active Twitter accounts. You should find many references to your niche on Twitter.com.Check Twitter accounts of people involved

within your niche and see how many followers they have (should be at least 2,000).

➤ Go to Twitter and do a search for [your niche].Are there any offline magazines? This is the gold standard for a niche. If somebody is going to the trouble and expense of creating a hard-copy magazine centered on your niche, you can be sure there are online fans looking for information about the topic. You can check Amazon Magazines or just do Google search for "[your niche] magazine or journal." In regards to our "golf tips" an example, we see all the golf-related magazines at the local grocery stores. If just one or two of these points are positive, it's a good sign your niche has a potential.

Find your monetization potential

Now you observed that can earn money with your blog? There are many people who start blogging as a hobby without necessary intention at monetizing their blog. Still, others want to make extra cash or even vision of make a living by blogging. It doesn't matter which category you're in, it wouldn't hurt to know if your blog can produce the income you desire. If you found other blogs, active social profiles and offline magazines or journals in the previous sections, this indicates the niche is active and possibly you can monetize it. More detail explanation about monetization techniques in Chapter 6.

How to make sure your niche is monitazable

Research the following:

> ➢ Is anyone selling information or products related to your niche? The easiest way to determine this is to see what products your competitors are promoting.

> ➢ Are there well-known advertisers in your niche? These could be the big brands or e-commerce sites.

> ➢ Are there any affiliate offers in your niche?.Here is how to find affiliate offers: Then Check affiliate networks such as (Clickbank.com, CJ.com and ShareSale.com and Amazon Affiliate).

> ➢ Do a Google search for "[your keyword] affiliate" or "[your keyword] affiliate program."

I am sure these points can help you determine if you can establish a blog in the niche of your choice that will helps you generate income.

What readers need from your blog.

What content do you want to start creating? You can write about anything and everything, but you have to make sure that you really understand what your readers want to see or read. While there may be other existing blogs dedicated to your area of expertise, they are not for you! If you have a unique perspective and approach, people will want to read about it. There's never enough information for the voracious appetites of collectors and enthusiasts. They always desire more and with practice, you can give them that.

Readers are looking for information

People who may visit your blog want to be informed. They want to learn or stay up to date on specific topics. You would be surprised what people are searching for online. For example, some people want news that doesn't appear in mainstream media. You can be the one to give what they desire.

Readers are looking for solutions

People always are searching for the solutions to their problems. Blogs solve a lot of problems in the world. Those problems might include dieting,health concerns, or how to prevent cancers. The Internet has become the world's largest library that anyone can benefit from. What can you add to the Internet? Your knowledge, experiences, and insights can help others.

Readers are looking to be entertained

The English proverb says all work without play makes a jack dull boy. So the Internet is not all work! People want to connect, laugh, and share with others. Your blog can quickly become popular for your brand of humor combined with the subject you choose. There are lots of fun information you can share with others that will help attract visitors to your blog.

How to choose a blogging platform

At this stage, in this 4th hour of starting your journey to become a blogger. You'll need to determine the blog-management platform you want to use. We recommend that you set up your blog on one of the self-hosted platforms. But before you make the decision, let us discuss each option below in more detail and talk about the pros and cons. For in-depth reviews of different blogging platforms. When it comes to starting your blog you have the following options:

- ➢ free,
- ➢ premium

➢   Self-hosted   platforms (recommended).

Important points to understand about blogging

As you continue to put time and energy into your blog, you will begin to see better, bigger returns on your investment. Depending on how you're planning to manage your blog, you'll need to consider the amount of time the work will require. Meanwhile, your blog is your online journal and you'll write a few paragraphs or articles a week. Or you might choose and update your content on a daily basis. But remember: It will take time to create your Web presence. Be patient, keep up the good work, and be consistent with your blogging.

Free platforms

For new bloggers, the availability of free blogging platforms such as Blogger or Tumblr is tempting. The benefits include being free and quick to start. But having a blog name in this form—yourname.tumblr.com   or yourname.blogspot.com is the sign of an inexpert beginner who likely won't be taken seriously.

If you keep your blog on a free platform, you let the platform own your name. You'll be subject to their rules and restrictions, they may limit or prohibit ads on your blog, or they may even place their own ads on your blog. If you're serious about blogging, you'll need to move away from this option.

Premium platforms

This is not free platforms, Premium means you'll have a trial period before you have to start paying (costs vary from $5 to $30 per month).Several platforms are available. One of the most popular is TypePad. This platform focuses on ease of use for writing, but customization options which are limited and it lacks certain features and of value to bloggers.By default, your TypePad blog name will look like this: yourname.typepad.com. It's not always the best option if you're trying to build the good name and brand for your blog. However, you could point your own domain (purchased through any domain registrar) to TypePad blog by applying domain mapping process.

Self-hosted platforms

Think wisely and own your blog! One of the best and most recognized self-hosted content management systems (CMS) is WordPress.org, also recommended by 90 percent of blogging experts we've surveyed.

Self-hosted platforms allow you to run a blog on your own domain. Aside from following your domain registrar and web hosting company's rules, you're in total control and fully in charge of your blog and its contents. You have a number of different choices when it comes to a self-hosted blog system (also called Content Management System or CMS).

The blog set up is called self-hosted because you will use your own web hosting spacelike (WebHostingHub) and name for your blog. This normally costs $5 to $10 per month for the web space (hosting account), depending on the company you choose, and $12 to $15 per year for the name(domain).The actual CMS is usually open-source and free.

Throughout this book, we'll be showing you how to start, manage, customize, and work with the WordPress CMS. By using our simple guides, you will be able to create your blog quickly and learn how to manage it in short order. We'll show you how to set up and go live with your WordPress blog in Chapter 2.

Point to remember

Whatever your choice and involvement, you should follow these few simple rules for your success:

> Choose your niche wisely and validate it before you move forward.

> Think about the content you can create to differentiate your blog from others.

> Select your blogging platform and get ready to launch your blog.

This is a time for your break. 20 hour left for you to become a successful blogger.

Chapter two

how to set up a self-hosted 5 hour

Wordpress Blog

In this chapter, you will learn the alpha and omega of creating your blog, including tips for choosing a domain name and web hosting options. We also provided a useful definition of terms. In the previous chapter, you have learned that a self-hosted WordPress blog is the best choice for most bloggers. If you want to get your new self-hosted blog started, you need to decide on two important things:

A domain name

A web hosting provider.

Domain name.

Your domain name represents you, your blog, your company, and your brand. Make it recognizable, easy to remember a proud symbol of you and your blog. For example,the strong domain names are amazon.com, apple.com, and Hi.com etc.

Web hosting.

After choosing good domain name, selecting reliable hosting services will be one of the most important aspects and decisions you make. The functionality and performance of your blog will depend on your hosting provider.The host company makes sure your blog is available 24/7 to potential readers and it is where your files are stored in the cloud online.

Most hosting companies offer domain registration services. Some people prepare to keep their domain name with the registrar company, separate from the hosting account.This book recommends keeping it all under your hosting account for peaceful management and maintenance.

What is a domain name?

Your domain name will be the address name by which you will be known online, no matter what niche you choose. It's the distinctive address of your blog on the Internet. Your domain will be yours as long as you continue paying the annual fee ($10 - $15 for .com domain).

Users who know your domain address,URL (uniform resource locator) can simply type it into their browser's address bar. Others people will be able to discover your blog through search engines such as Google and Bing, so you definitely need to find a unique name called Moniker. Make sure you love your original domain name because you'll face a number of some challenges if you decide to change it down the road.

Types of domain names

Just as you and your business have a physical address, your domain name also needs one too. It may be the popular "dot com" or it may be a country or niche specific. From .us (United States) to .co.uk (United Kingdom) and from.guru (yes, for life coaches)to .sport (for sports-related domains), these top-level domains (TLDs) are added to any domain name and organize it to point to their location. The general rule in this is to go for a "dot com" domain, but some of the other extensions can work. like "dot net" or "dot me."In the end, it's about being memorable and brandable, so if a different extension or country code helps you be memorable, then break the rules!.

How to select a blog name

Can you remember the anxiety of naming your first pet? It's the same with naming your blog. It's a name directly tied to you. You'll be fashionable, teased, or forgotten because of it, so choose wisely. The rules we've mentioned previously, as well as those listed below, will give you some great ideas on how to select and formulate the perfect domain name.

Rules for choosing the right domain name

Start by brainstorming

You can pick at least five main words or phrases that describe your blog topic. Write them down, then mix and match these words to create new domain names. Choose the one that sounds good and will be memorable. There's a rule in advertising strategy that says when launching a new product, you need to start by making a list of 10 names. The first three are easy. Maybe you can do five or six without breaking a sweat, but by the time you get to last one, you'll be stuck for more ideas. Using the outline described above, pick the best one from your list and you are on your way to becoming a successful blogger.

2. Choose unique name

Choice unique name using a search engine,like Google, search out your planned blog name. If your search shows any sites with similar names? If it does, then make sure you try a different name.Giving your blog a name that's similar to other existing sites is the first step to failure. Additionally, do not choose names that are plural or misspelled versions of existing sites.

3. Make it easy to type

Do not make it that you have to spell the name out more than once, it won't work. Keep the name as easy, and simple to remember and type in a search field or address bar as possible. You don't want your future visitors to incorrectly type in your name and they can be directed to a totally different site. A typical example of this is a popular social site called Flickr.com, was started in 2005.Four years later, the company had to acquire another domain name called Flicker.com for a large amount of money in order to redirect visitors who misspelled their name. But if you're determined to have that oddly spelled name, then make sure the domain names for common misspellings are available as well, so you can register both of them and redirect visitors to the main domain.

4. Choose dot com first

More than 55 percent of all websites are "dot.com" domains. It's still the preferred extension and the easiest to remember. If your top name choice in your list isn't available, then try your second choice before accepting another TLD. Remember that some browsers on Windows and Mac os accept address-only entries in their address bar. If you type just the domain name without the extension (and who knows how many of your users will just do that?) they will return, by default, to the .com site.

5. Make it brandable

It is better to make your domain name represents your brand. Some names speak for themselves—when you hear the name, you know what the blog is about, example once you see the site that name cars.com. I am sure your mind can decide what the site is all about

6. Shorter is always better

As we've mentioned before, shorter is better. If you can't get your domain name down to one memorable word (almost impossible to come in present days), then consider adding one, or at maximum, two more words. Combinations of two words work great for the memorable names like Autocar.com or GeekSquad.com. It is very imperative that you should not use an acronym. People rarely remember the letters unless it's an exceptionally catchy name.

7. Avoid trademark problem

Once you've selected your top choices for your blog name, you have to make sure you're not violating anyone's trademarks. To check this within the US, visit uspto.gov/ trademarks and do the search before you register the name. This problem is not that regular for bloggers, but it's always good to check now because this could kill a great blog and business down the road. Also, if you are going to create a blog about a big-name product, like WordPress or Facebook, please try to review their terms and conditions. Most will not allow you to use their name in any part of your domain.

8. No numbers and hyphens

Numeral numbers and hyphens (especially hyphens) can cause confusion. Avoid them at all cost. Even something as clever as the number 2blogger.com will cause confusion. Make the name speak for itself.

9. It's not good to follow new trends

It's not always good to follow new trends. Anything that deals with something trendy will, like the trend, fade away. Stick with a classic name that will span the decades and not be dying down to a trend or fad.

10. Marry your domain name

You have to be 100% sure that you love your domain name. Once it's set, you'll be wedded to it for years to come. If you decide later to rename it, then you will lose time, money, brand equity and rankings. We do not recommend changing your domain once your blog has been live long enough to have gained many people that are following.

11. Check social network

You should know that, before you register your desired domain name, it's always a good idea to check social networks and see if the same name is being used. To keep your blog name constant and to build your brand, you want a name that is readily available. For example, check facebook.com/your domain, twitter.com/your domain and secure them as well. You can search for KnowEm is a great tool to use to see if certain names are already branded on social platforms.

Premium domain names 6 hour

You might find out that a domain name that's already taken, but not necessarily in use. These are usually referred to as premium domain names. They are domains registered by someone else and offered for sale to any customer. There's no way of telling you how much a domain is worth on the market, especially if you're after a niche domain.To buy a registered domain, check one of the auction sites: Godaddy Auction, Sedo, NameJet or SnapNames. If it's not for sale through auctions, you can contact the domain owner to see if you can make an offer to buy it. You can use Whois Tool to find the domain owner's details contact information. Even if the owner's name is protected or private, you can send an email to the provided email address on Whois and ultimately reach the domain owner.

What is web hosting?

I hope you are getting me right, now I will show you the way to choose a web hosting company to register. The domain name with and sign up for the hosting account to host your new blog online.The web hosting company provides you with space on a server to store your log files. It's similar to your personal computer files, except that your blog files are available online where visitors can access them at all times, by entering your domain name or by discovering your blog in a search engine. You can use free blogging platforms (as described in Chapter 1) and adopt with the restrictions, or take the leap and launch your own self-hosted blog, which 9 percent of top bloggers recommend.

How to choose a web-hosting provider

The wrong web host can cause problems with your blog. Just imagine choosing a mobile company that has no good network reception. Your web host is a major piece of the database to maintaining a successful blog, therefore, it's very important that you choose a reliable provider. When people are asked what services most important to look for in a good web host, they cite things like 24/7 phone and customers support, reliability, and reputation. Good hosting providers offer additional features such as database support, backup's clouds, and free email. Most hosting companies always offer similar options and features to a beginning blogger; you will not have to go intensely into technical details to use them.

Checklist for better web host selection

1. Good reputation

The rule of thumb for the web host selection is to check the website of the service provider for signs that indicate credibility. Such as a physical address, phone number, general company information and user positive reviews. Ask yourself this question "Would I trust and give this company my personal information? Also, check if the company is listed with Better Business Bureau; if they are listed, what is their rating?

2. Support

If you are the novice to the Internet, you might need to learn more on your web host's tech support. Look for a company that offers 24/7 support.(If you have any problem with your blog at 2 a.m., do you really want to wait for help?)Some companies offer real-time phone and chat support, others do not have these services. In lieu of on-call support and wait for a response. Many are specifically looking for U.S.-based support call support, a number of web hosting services only offer online ticket-based support. This means you submit a ticket since some providers use outsourced support. My recommendation here, Your best bet is to find a hosting company that offers 24/7 phone support in addition to online chats and support tickets

1. Uptime efficiency

As mentioned previously, it's important for your blog to be available online with no break in service. But when you're dealing with software and people, things can still go wrong. Most reliable companies have excellent technology in place to make sure your site is up and running all the time. The current industry standard for the good companies is "99 percent network uptime."Do more your own online search "[company name] uptime" and check for a provider's uptime listing and ranking.

2. Money-back guarantee

Some companies offer full money-back guarantees for a limited period of time (usually 30, 45 or 90 days). You might see" anytime money-back guarantee" claims from some companies. That usually means that you'll get a prorated amount back after the limited-time period passes. Ensure you read their "Terms of Service."

3. Features list

Do you know CMS, are you thinking of a specific CMS (content management system),such as our much-championed Wordpress? Does your prospective host provider offer it? The list of features can be long, but the more options for you the better. You might not need some of the listed features now, but once your blog grows bigger there could be a need for additional items.

4. Email accounts

Most host providers will give you the option of having unlimited email accounts for your blog.Having several email addresses is an advantage that can help you manage communication with your blog visitors. For example, you might have personal addresses name@yourdomain.com.

(sales@yourdomain.com)

(webmaster@yourdomain.com

admin@yourdomain.com). You should double check to make sure at least one email account is available for your domain.

5. Price

First-time customer fees for hosting services normally are reasonable and affordable as low as a few dollars per month for the first year of service. But you need to understand that subsequent year's renewal price will be different. Before choosing your provider, double check the renewal price information on the web host's website for more detail.

8. Site backup

Web host servers are not 100 percent protected. Data loss is possible, as it is on your own computer. After all, servers are big computers that everyone can read files from. You must backup both your site files and your databases. If they don't offer backup, you will be left with an option to figure out and do it manually. So make sure your host provider features an automated-backup option but a small monthly fee might be applied.

9. Scalability and room to grow

What happens when your blog becomes bigger? It's excellent to know your host can provide you with different hosting plan options. When your blog starts to grow and gets a lot more traffic and visitors, you might need to upgrade more power and speed. Think ahead and plan for a bright future for your blog!

10. Security

Your blog can hold a lot content of information. The threat of site hackers reminds us of the need for increasing your security. Most of the time it will be your responsibility to ensure you set up have secure passwords.But even then, malware and hackers can still strike, which can lead to havoc and downtime for your blog. Some hosting providers offer security-monitoring services for an extra charge.

11.Third-party security

Third-party providers, like VaultPress and Sucuri, can provide these backup and security services for you. You'll need to compare these costs, combined with your hosting company's monthly fee. Check the feasibility if it makes sense to go with a cheaper solution and third-party security or a more expensive hosting solution that has these services built into their fees.

Instructions for setting up a blog 7 Hour

Now it's time to get your domain name, web hosting account and set up your new blog. This is 7th hour of your successful blogging. You will find action steps you need to take and easy-to-follow guide to get your blog set up with trusted hosting providers (we prefer WebHostingHub). If you choose to go with a different hosting company, the setup process might be slightly different but the action steps will be the same.

Action steps

1. Get resisted domain & hosting

Sign up for a reliable hosting account to get started.

2. Install Wordpress CMS

3. Your own blog is live

Welcome to the Web! You can start blogging instantly.

Words of wisdom before you start your blogging journey.

We have mentioned about some of these points already in Chapter 1, but let's do a reiterate since they're worth repeating. When you create a blog, you need to future-proof it in order to ensure there will not be any big obstacles in your way. Your vision needs to be the long-term plan. Decisions you make today can change your online presence in the future. The following information will help you to avoid these mistakes, saving your time and money.

1. Make sure your blog topic is viable

You know there is an audience for every niche, there may be fewer than 30 people looking for the specific topic you want to cover within your niche. Check the existing competition. If you see other blogs covering that same of your topic, it means there is a demand for that information. There are a lot of great ideas that were ahead of their time and ones that want to be discovered. Make sure you differentiate your idea and make it attractive to others.

2. Don't be afraid of technology

We understand some of this technical talk is a bit intimidating. You may be nervous and think you'll never get it right, but you're wrong. We had a 60-year-old client who didn't know anything about blogs but publishing his own in no time. He went from not being able to program a VCR to become a blogging expert in his field. If you follow the steps we provide in this book, you'll see it's as easy as clicking a button.

3. You may not have to be a web designer

In this book, we'll show you how to set up your blog without any previous knowledge of coding and how you can make it a great-looking blog without Web design skills.

Be patient and give it time

It will take time to establish your Web presence. But we assure you that within 24 hours you can become a successful blogger. Be prepared to wait and be consistent with the step by step guidance. Set a few pieces of content on a scheduled publishing date so you can step away for a long weekend without blogging. Get right back to it when you return home. And remember that good thing come to those who wait. You will get to the top gradually so be patient.

Congratulations for owning your blog

We mentioned some free blog-hosting options, the best call to action is to own your blog, especially if you will be using your own copyrighted material(articles,drawings, photos). You can pay a small amount of money every month, and you will build your own equity. Dealing with a hosting provider is a profession

Chapter three

How to use wordpress for blogging 8 hour

In this 8 hour, we will take a closer look at managing your WordPress blog. You are going to learn how to customize your blog, make design and layout changes, create your first post or page and much more.

Wordpress front and back ends

The WordPress platform consists of two main areas: your blog's front end and back end. The front end is what your visitors will always see when they come to your blog. Many of the tasks performed on the back end will be visible on the front end, such as theme customizations, plugin functionality enhancements, and content publication. You can perform some actions with your visitors directly from the front end of the blog, including comments and social sharing. The back end is called the WordPress dashboard, allow you to fully manage your blog's content, community, functionality, and design. It is accessible only by users who you designate and assigns account managers on your blog. For you to access your WordPress dashboard, you need to type: example.com/ wp-admin in the address bar of your browser and log in using your WordPress username and password.

Navigating the dashboard

The Dashboard is the core of blog administration. It consists of three main parts:

> ➤ Left side menu.

> ➤ Top toolbar.

> ➤ Middle section.

The left-hand side column

The left-hand of your WordPress dashboard is where you'll find all of your admin options and where most of your creative effort will be focused. This column includes menu options with their icons for each of the following functional areas:

1. Updates

Find updates to the WordPress platform along with plug-in and themes you have already installed.

2. Posts

To View, all posts (blog content), add a new post, view, and create categories, view and create tags.

3. Media

To view your media library (images, documents, and other file uploads) and upload new files.

4. Pages

To view and add new static pages to your

5. Blog.Comments

Manager-comment is where you will approve or delete new comments on blog posts and pages.

6. Appearance

Manage themes, customize your blog design (dependent upon theme), manage widgets, manage menu items, and edit your blog's header (dependent upon theme).

7. Plugins

Manage and add new plugins to enhance WordPress functionality.

8. Users

Manage users, add new users, and update your WordPress profile (name, password, and details).

9. Tools

Tools to import and export content to and from your WordPress blog.

10. Settings

Edit a general blog setting, which includes writing settings, reading settings, discussion (comment) settings, media settings, and permalinks (URL formatting for your blog).

In addition to the general menu items in the left-hand column mentioned above, you will also find menu options for plugins you have installed. Depending on the plugin's purpose, it's settings can be added to any standard menu(posts, pages, comments, appearance, plugins, users, tools or settings) or as a new menu item anywhere in the left-hand column.

The dashboard   9 Hour

Updates

WordPress is like other popular CMS, releases both minor and major updates to their platform in order to launch new features, fix bugs and increase security. In the past, you would be given an opportunity to update to the latest version of WordPress. It is done through your Dashboard using a one-click install process or by downloading the latest version and installing it yourself.For any blogger who has WordPress 3.7 or above, can easily update to the core WordPress platform are installed automatically on your website. But you are still responsible for updating your plugin and themes when updates become available. If you don't like WordPress to automatically update the core of their platform, you can find directions on how to configure automatic updates in the WordPress Codex.

Posts

The Posts menu will allow you to control the new content you add to your blog. Your blog posts published in descending order (newest first).In the Posts menu, you will find the following options.

➤All Posts: A list all of your posts in the dashboard. You can use the listing to swiftly edit single or multiple post categories, tags, status, author, and ability to comment.

➤ Add New: This is where you can add a new post to your blog.

➤ Categories: To view all of the categories your posts are listed under, edit them and add new categories.

➤Tags: To view all of the keywords your posts are tagged with, edit them and add new tags.

Media

Your WordPress installation comes with an exclusive media manager. With it; you can upload rich media content and assign it to posts, pages, sidebars, and header. Everything from photos and videos and audio files. Your media files can be previewed added, edited or deleted. In the Media menu, you will find the following options.

➤ Library:To view all of the media uploaded to your WordPress blog.

> ➢ Add New: To Add new media to your WordPress blog.

Pages

Pages provide stationary content or information to the readers.Standard pages that bloggers use include About, Contact, Advertise, Products, Services, and Resources. The following options are available on the Pages menu bar, you will find the following options.

> ➢All Pages: A list of all pages in the dashboard. You can use the listing quickly edit single or multiple pages' status, author, parent, template, and ability to comment.

> ➢Add New: Add new pages to your blog.

Posts and pages

Your blog content will be displayed in pages and posts. However, they have similarities, but they serve different purposes and have different behaviors.

They have the following in common:

➢A title/headline and specific content

➢Meta information (author, date of publishing)

➢They can be added, deleted, updated, or edited.

➢ They will be available for everyone or only a limited number of users based on your choice of settings.

➢ They can contain anything from plain text to media-rich content (video, audio, photo, links, etc.).

➢They can be altered or extended via plugins.

The difference between posts and pages

➢Pages are not a part of your main blog's content. For example, if you have a sports blog, you would write posts about your latest sports event. You would reserve pages for things that relate to you and the blog, such as a page with information about you or a page with a contact form to contact you.

➤ Posts are part of your main blog's content. They will show up as new entries inside your blog and your RSS feed (Rich Site Summary is a web feed used to share out information from your blog to subscribers).Your pages will only be displayed when you link them directly and never within your RSS feed.

Comments

The Comments feature is the greatest way to manage reader interaction. It allows readers to add comments on the topic, ask questions and provide feedback. It allows your readers to stay engaged with the community and interact with your specific niche market. Both blog posts and pages can allow comments. Most of the WordPress themes come equipped with comment layout functionality. However, it is your responsibility to engage with your readers and encourage them to leave comments on your blog. Check for new comments regularly and approve them promptly and reply to them instantly. In the Comments section, you have the ability to moderate comments, including approving them, marking them as spam or delete them entirely.

Appearance 10 hour

This menu is where most of the activity of changing the design and layout of your blog takes place. On appearance menu, you can search for and install new themes and make additional customizations to your blog's header image, colors and background. In the Appearance menu, you will find the following options: (We're only presenting options that are commonly available. Keep in mind that options will vary, depending on the theme you choose.)

The Appearance menu contains the following options:

> ➢ Themes -You may search for themes on the WordPress network or install themes you have downloaded

from elsewhere.We will talk about theme selection method shortly.

➢ Customize - Use the Customize section to make any changes to the theme's design in a visual editor. Items that can be customized are: Title and Tagline, Color, Background Image, Static

Front Page and Featured Content.

➢Widgets - Widgets are boxes you can add to various areas of WordPress blog.Depending on the theme you've chosen, this can consist of the homepage, header, sidebar, and footer. Adding widgets is a simple task by the use of a drag & drop process. Widgets can display social media links, a search bar, subscription links, "About" text for the blog, most recent posts, most recent comments, and links to other blogs that go together with yours.

➢ Menus - Create one or more menus that will appear horizontally in your header.

➢ Header-Upload any graphic at a specific size (determined by your theme) which will be displayed at the top of your blog.

➢ Background - Change background colors or upload your own background image.

➢ Editor- The editor is for advanced users and involves a knowledge of coding. It gives you the option of editing theme code for specific functionality and design changes. Visitors will be able to immediately see any changes that you save in your theme's code, it's usually safer to edit copies of your files offline, test them, and upload your changes when they are verified. If you are going to use the Editor, always make sure you back-up a current version of your blog before editing your files. If there is any problem, you can always upload a previous version of the code to fix it.

Blog design and layout

The first thing your blog's front end needs is a good face (design and layout).You want to create an environment that is eye-catching. In the long run, you want your visitors to easily find information on your blog. You don't want visitors to be downcast by the colors you choose or the non-intuitive and unpractical way in which information is displayed. Your design can cause instant distrust of your blog or instant acceptance.Start your search for a good theme as soon as your WordPress platform is installed. The look and feel of your blog rely on the theme you choose. Your blog visitor will first notice the overall appearance of the blog, before even taking a look at the content. Choose a theme that looks great, but also works for your unique content needs. The default theme that comes with your WordPress blog installed is 2014.However, it is a good for starter theme, but if you want to choose a theme that is more unique to your blog and compatible with your niche.

Checklist for choosing your theme

By searching within blog dashboard:

➢ Read the description

Most themes come with a little description of features and functionality. By reading it, you should have an estimate if the theme matches your blog needs and how customizable it is.

➢ Check the ratings

Popular themes will have star ratings that are visible in the preview and under theme details description. They should give you a clear idea how good the theme is.

➢ Preview the theme

To preview the theme, to get an idea of the overall look and layout.

➢ Check for responsiveness

The Aim for a responsive design is that it will work on desktop browsers and mobile devices.

If you discover a theme that takes your breath away, cool down. Once you install a theme you be fond of, don't be surprised if it doesn't look quite right. Your theme is just a skeleton of your blog. To make it appealing, you'll have to fill in other content(text,photos, videos, etc.).Earlier, we showed you how to add content to your blog.

Premium and custom themes   11 hour

➤ Free theme

For many visionary beginner bloggers, the world is not enough. The stash of free themes (more than 2000 themes are available on wordpress.org) does not satisfy their particular desire for look and feel. There are two options you can take a look at, premium and custom themes. But they a cost for it, sometimes a tiny one, at other times a huge amount.

➤ Premium themes

The premium theme is created by both single developers and some showcase websites.Top sources for premium themes that are worth checking include StudioPress, Elegant Themes,Themefuse, Thesis, WooThemes, and ThemeForest. The price range for a single-user license ranges from $50 to $500,depending on which premium theme you choose.

➤ Custom themes

Custom themes are created by an individual developer (coder and designer) who will either customize an existing theme or create a brand new theme for you. They are not the ideal choice for beginner bloggers due to their high cost. Prices to customize a themed range from $600 to $2,000, depending on the features you want.

Based on our experience, we recommend you the following free and premium themes for new bloggers.

Free themes

1.   Decode is a top free choice for bloggers who are after a minimal look. Customizations include different colors and sidebar items accessible from the main menu.

2.   Supernova, even though its classical blog looks and feel, is a true gem. With color palettes, full-width sliders and custom headers.

3.   Clean Retina is a simple, clean, and responsive theme that adapts automatically to any browser size. Along with the elegant design, the theme is easily customizable.

➢ Premium themes

You can find different premium themes online from the resources mentioned earlier.This book recommends you to check the themes series from:

➢ StudioPress. Their services and support are top and all of their cost themes are highly customizable. Here are three themes that are suited for the blog.

➢ Wintersong is a theme that carries an air of the bare essentials.Calm, minimal, and outstanding,it's versatile enough to work for all types of sites.

➢ Beautiful is a theme that shows a lot of attention to details,you can customize to give your website a unique look.

➢ Modern Blogger theme is bold, sleek and colorful. With a current look than meets the needs of the passionate blogger.

Advanced customizations   12 Hour

Now, look at the areas in your WordPress dashboard where you can do most of your blog customizations.

Plugin

Plug-in is basic bundled pieces of code that affect the way your blog looks or feels.They can add some new functionality to your blog, extend your theme's capabilities and customize your blog as a whole or in part. While most of the plug-in is free, there is plenty that is offered for a fee based on their unique functionality.

Recommended plug-in for new bloggers

Remember this is the 12th hour to your journey to becoming a successful blogger.for the sake of time management, let's save you time, we've compiled some important plug-in for your immediate blogging needs. They cover many aspects of your blogging experience, improving the functionality of your blog and make it more professional and attractive to your readers.

1. Google Analytics

The top and best choice when it comes to monitoring and analyzing your website traffic.

2. Contact Form 7

The contact form comes with flexible email options.

3. Digg Digg

A floating or static palette with social media and sharing options.

4. Disqus Commenting System

A substitute to the basic WordPress comment system with advanced administrative and comment capabilities.

5. Yoast SEO

A comprehensive SEO plug-in for your blog.The best free SEO plug-in system.

6. WP Super Cache

Increases speeds up the load time of your WordPress blog.

7. Akismet

This provides Protection from comment spam(you won't need this if you go with Disqus for comments).

8. YARPP

This plug-in automatically creates a "related posts" list at the end of each of your posts, to encourage people to continue browsing your site.

9. Authors Widget

This is a great way to display multiple authors and their activity on your blog-site.

Supplementary menu options

1. Users

Users section allows you to add new users to your WordPress blog, modify your own user profile and edit users you have added to your WordPress blog. You can assign each user one of the following roles.

2. Administrator

The administrator is the blog manager that performs all actions on the blog. This should be better reserved for you as the site owner and only those you trust highly with your blog. Administrators have the ability to perform all the actions you can. So they can even lock you out of your own site!

3. Editor

The editor can access and edit all blog posts, pages, comments, categories, tags, and links.

4. Author

This can be any person that can publish and edit articles, posts and upload media.

5. Contributor

They write and edit their own posts, but are not able to publish without your consent.

6. Subscriber

They can only read and comment on posts or pages.

Tools

These Tools can help you to able to execute some extended tasks on your WordPress blog.

1. Available tools

This section comes with the pre-installed option called "Press This" that provides a fast and easy way to clip text, images, and videos from any site and share them on your blog.Under "Press This," there is also a categories-to-tags converter.

2. Import tool

This enables you to import data from other blogging platforms into your WordPress.

3. Export tool

This enables you to export blog content which can later be imported into a new WordPress installation. It is a very useful way to back up your blog content.

4. Settings

This setting menu contains all of the settings options for your WordPress site.

5. General

This menu configures basic options for your WordPress site, including the site name, description, URL, time zone, date format and main administrator email.

6. Writing

Allow you to set default categories and post formats for your content. WordPress will automatically assign a category and format if you don't.

7. Reading

This set the home page for your site (either a static page or the latest blog posts), the number of blog posts on your homepage and all archives, the number of items in your RSS feed, and whether you want to show your full post or a synopsis in your RSS feed.

8. Discussion

Here you can control how comments are received on your blog. The normal setting is to moderate all new-comment authors and automatically approve comments by previously approved comment authors. It's very important to hold in moderation comments with multiple links as this is a sign of a spammer.

9. Media

With media, you customize the default sizes for images uploaded to your blog.

10. Permalinks

This allows you to customize the URL structure for your blog.The best choice is to have a structure that allows keywords from your post/page titles to be implemented into your URL, also known as the post name structure.

Congratulation!!!

Remember you are now completed 12 hours; you have come to the half-way through your journey to become a successful blogger. You should have learned every section of your Dashboard and get comfortable with the management options. Doing so will allow you to improve your blog's design, functionality, and personality. Once you know how to customize your blog, make the necessary tweaks, and make it stand out and please your readers.

Chapter four

how to create great blog content hour 13

Now that you have your blog set up, your next goal is to write and create content. The content of your blog will be the enticement that attracts your readers. In this chapter, on 13 hours to become a successful blogger. We will cover what the content your blog consists of, the types of content you can create and blogging practices you should follow. Any blog without great content, even the most well designed, tightly structured blogs will ultimately fail.

Types of content you need to create for your blog.

➢ Pages content comprises of static page content, such as "About" and "Contact."

➢ Sidebar content contains static content that appears on the sidebar of your blog.

➢ Blog posts contain regular posts about your niche.

Prior to start writing your day-to-day "Blog posts" you will need to make sure the static "Pages" and "Sidebar" content of your blog is created and uploaded to your blog.

Let's explain each of these content areas.

1. Pages content

First, you will need to create static content pages for the following types of information.

➢ About

The good number traditional page on any blog is the about page. This page tells new visitors to your blog what it is about, who you are, and why you have a blog about your specific topic. Depending on your chosen niche and your style, the information you provide can be "all business" or personal and fun.

➢ Contact

This page enables any visitors to your blog to contact you at any time. It can be a simple page with your email address plus social network links or you can use plugins like Contact Form 7 to have a contact form visitors that can use to contact you without leaving your website.

➢ Products and services –

If you created your blog to promote your business, you'll want to make sure there's a page has the details of products or services you sell. On the other hand, if you already have a website for your business, you can provide a link to it in your menu.

➢ Disclaimer/policy –

To give your blog a little liability protection, you might want to consider a disclaimers or policy page. For example, if you are writing a health blog, but you are not a medical professional, you may create a disclaimer to say that you are not a physician or other healthcare professional and recommend that readers should see their doctors for their personal medical information and evaluation. You may want to also inform visitors to your website that you use analytics tracking, Google AdSense, affiliate marketing links and other types of content.

When your blog continues to grow,you will also want to consider adding the following pages.

> Pillar pages

When you add new content to your blog, you will want to consider creating pillar pages.These are pages that direct visitors to your blog to particular posts on specific topics.

> Archives

This page guides people to your most recent posts, main categories, top tags and content you have created that's not located on your blogs, such as guest posts, interviews, podcasts, and videos etc,

> Advertising page

If you want to start advertising on your blog and you have enough traffic to make it worthwhile for advertisers, you may create an advertising page that shows off your latest stats (number of website visitors, page views, email subscribers, RSS subscribers, etc.).

Make sure to visit other blogs in your niche. Preferably the prominent one, to see what pages they provide links for in their main navigation bar, sidebar, and footer. Chances are, your visitors will be looking for the same types of pages on your blog.

2. Sidebar content

The sidebar is the smaller column to the left or right (depending on the theme you selected) of your blog's main content. You can add the following content in sidebar widgets for your visitors.

➢ Subscribe

Encourage all visitors to your blog to subscribe via email or RSS.Email, of course, is best, especially if you would like to monetize your blog in the future. MailChimp is a grand service and it's free for the first 2,000 subscribers.

➢ About

This is a simple sentence about you and your blog for new visitors who may not take the time to read your About page.Put your photo in this blurb of text helps visitors put a face to the blog, whether you are the owner and editor managing other writers, or the main content author.

➢ Follow

Below your about widget, you will want to display links to your social profiles so people can follow you. Generally, this will be your Facebook page, Twitter profile, and Google+ profile/page. You can also use icons to represent each network or use official boxes, buttons, and badges from these networks. This will help you build your social media audience by allowing people to connect with you without leaving your website.

➤ Popular Posts

A Popular Posts widget will direct visitors to your top content. The WordPress Popular Posts plugin will help you create this easy, displaying posts based on comments and view count.

➤ Advertisers

If you plan to add advertising banners to your blog, then add them from the beginning so regular visitors will not be surprised when you do start gaining advertisers. The banners you use until they can link to products for which you are an affiliate marketer or to products you simply need to sell.

Blog post content basics

One technical element of blog posts that every blogger in every niche needs to stick.

Create good content with readers in mind.

You should learn about optimizing your content for search engines, and it is important, if you don't optimize your blog content for humans, then you'll never gain the exposure that it takes to eventually get links and rank well in search engines. If you write good content that people love to read, then you will get traffic, social shares and links as your readership grows.

Basic components of a blog post

The following are basic elements of a great blog post. We will talk about how to design each, for both readers and search engines.

> ➢ Headline

The headline can be your title of your blog post. It must be created to capture the attention of potential readers who may see it in their social media newsfeeds or in search results. Make sure you've found a great keyword phrase that people searching will use to find blog posts on your topic—and include it in your headline.

> ➢ Introduction

The first paragraph is very important for your blog post. It will either keep people reading or make people leave. Ensure that it compels people to read the rest of your content. You must use your targeted keyword phrase for search at least once in this paragraph.

> Main content

This is the main segment of your blog post content. Think of the headline as the guarantee and the main content as the fulfillment of that promise. Your main content should be the first point to satisfy anyone who visits your post based on the headline. If you create bad content that does not satisfy the promises of your headline, people will start to identify your blog as unfulfilling and thus, stop visiting. The length of your blog posts can be from 300 to 3,000 or more words. It is good to alternate the length of your posts as you gain insight into what works best for your audience.

> Subheads (Sub-headlines)

Many visitors will scan your blog content as opposed to reading it word for word. You should write subheads that break your content into digestible sections and make sure those subheads represent the content within them.

> Bold text

Always use bold text in a few areas of your main content to help highlight important points. Use it selectively; otherwise, the entire article will seem bolded, thus taking away the ability to highlight key portions of content.

> Bulleted/numbered lists

You do not allow your entire post to be bulleted or numbered lists, these lists to help separate out steps and lists with useful content.

> Media

Complement the text portion of your content with media, such as relevant images and video. This will help up your content and illustrate your points better. Images can also be used as part of the search optimization of your blog post. Input your post's main keyword phrase in the filename of the image as well as the ALT tag.

> Conclusion

The conclusion should be a paragraph at the end of your post to summarize what the reader should have gotten out of it.If they didn't, chances are, they will go back to see what they might have missed in the body content.

> Call to action

The last written line of your blog post should be some form of a call to action. It may be as simple as asking readers to share their thoughts in the comments or to share the post on social media if they enjoyed it. If your post is written to promote a particular product or service, the call to action should encourage the reader to learn more about it. But remember, You don't have to include all of the elements mentioned from this list in every post, but make sure you always have an engaging introduction, quality content, and a solid conclusion.

Types of blog content   14 hour

This is 14 hour to become the successful blogger. We assume that now can call yourself a blogger. But you don't have to be limited to standard blog posts to share your expertise. Here is the list of various content types you can use to supplement your blog content. The best part about these types of content is that you don't have to create unique content if you want to explore different formats.You can take any podcast transcription and turn it into a blog post. You can take several blog posts and joint them together into an eBook.

1. Podcasts

If you want to speak or interview others, then podcasts should be part of your content. They allow you to gain new readers from those who love podcasts, and you may transcribe or summarize your podcasts in blog posts.

2. Infographics

For those with design ability, infographics can be a great way to get more exposure for your ideas. With precision design and backed-up facts, you can get your content featured on sites that regularly post infographics.

3. EBooks

EBooks are great freebies for building your email list or, alternatively, something you can sell on your website and Amazon Kindle.You can generate them from scratch or repackage several blog posts that cover a specific theme.

4. Videos

If you want to get new visitors from YouTube, or simply feel it's easier to record a video than write a blog post, the video content should be in your plans. All you need is an HD camera,a microphone and/or a good screen capture program like Screenflow. Nevertheless, if you want to record tutorials from your computer,you can also create videos from Google+ hangouts and other platforms.

5. Presentations

Can you enjoy creating PowerPoint presentations or Prezis? Then create slideshow content that you can use on sites like Slideshare to complement your blog content.

6. Whitepapers & Case Studies

If your choice to write in-depth, researched content, then consider whitepapers and case studies. These can be summarized in a blog post, and then offered them for a free download to build your email list or in exchange for social shares.

Best blogging practices   15 hour

The following are great point stated for you to become a successful blogger in any niche. You have to follow these best practices.

1. Set your blogging goals

If you are getting the most out of your blogging, you have to set goals for your blog. Is your goal to make money? Get a new job? Find different people to connect with about a specific topic? Define your blogging goals and occasionally ask yourself if your blog is helping you meet them. If not, ask yourself how you can improve your blog in order to meet the stated goals.

2. Commit to becoming an expert

No matter how your blogging goals are, if you strive to be an expert in your niche, the fulfillment of your goals is certain to follow. People who are known as experts in their niche tend to receive more respect and income for their content. They tend to have many audiences and the option to turn their readers into customers by offering related products and services.

3.   Engage with your audience

The best way to stay with your readers is to engage with them. Several ways to do this include replying to comments, responding to queries from your contact form, joining in conversations with readers on social media networks, and visiting your readers' blogs to see what they are interested in and join their discussions. As you do this diligently, you will build stronger relationships with your readers and learn more about what they want, something that can help inspires your future content.

4.   You should be consistent and realistic

Creating a consistent time of posting on your blog helps your readers know when they can expect to hear from you again, whether it's daily, weekly, fortnightly, and monthly or even quarterly. The key is to maintaining consistency. One individual blogger will find it difficult to create high-quality content on a daily basis. Start with weekly or bi-weekly posts and work your way up to daily posts, if that is your ultimate goal. Remember, don't sacrifice quantity for quality.

5. Use an editorial calendar

What will help you to maintain your consistency, ensure to use some form of the editorial calendar? You can use Google Calendar, Outlook Calendar, and a simple spreadsheet. Use it to manage your ideas and plan your content themes for each month so that blogging is something you focus on, but not something you do in your spare time.

Proofread and edit your work

For many people, it's difficult to create content. Then it is very important to proofread and edit it.As a matter of fact, editing while writing can hinder your creative flow.

Proofreading is not optional. A blog post full of misspelled words and typos reflects poorly on you. If you're not capable to do these tasks on your own, consider hiring a virtual assistant to do it for you. This is particularly important if you're not writing in your native language. Having a native speaker of the language used in your blog edit your work can boost your credibility. While blog content does not need to be 100 percent perfect; it does need to be easy to read and consume.

Analyze your data

Make sure to install Google Analytics when you begin blogging and regularly check your data. In general, you want to make sure that, your traffic is growing and see which websites, social networks and other types of sources drive the most visitors to your blog. You should also watch for significant drops in traffic, as these drops may indicate a bigger problem, such as downtime for your website or loss of traffic due to Google algorithm changes.

Congratulation once again

Now you have spent 15 hours to become a successful blogger. If you want your blog to expand thrive and grow, and then you must be creating quality content that's compelling to your readers is the answer. Focus on quality over quantity, even if you have to sacrifice frequency and consistency. Always your readers' value content that's relevant, factual and   timely.

Chapter five

how to promote your blog hour 16

In chapter 4, you have learned that your blog content is the defining factor that will make or break your blog. You learned what it takes to create marvelous content, as well as the types of content you can create for your audience. However, your content alone will never help you succeed in blogging if no one ever sees it.

This is the reason why you need to learn online marketing strategies to help you market your blog as a whole, as well as each piece of content you create. This is known as content marketing. Your content marketing skills will determine how the traffic comes to your website, how many social shares you receive, how many comments you have made on your posts and how many subscribers you gain. Finally, the goal is to have as many visitors as possible when you start to monetize your blog. Visitors who you may convert into advertising clicks, affiliate referrals, and product/service buyers. Depending on your monetization strategy, which will be discussed in chapter 6.Until then, let us see the ways you can promote your blog and your content.

Get ready for promotion

Anyways, before you start promoting your blog, you should make sure it's ready. This step is for checking everything you have done from beginning of your first hour to this 16 hour. Start from setting up your blog, to creating your pages and posts.

➢Make sure your blog core content is live and ready for promotion.

➢Test your menu bar and sidebar links to make sure everything from pages, posts, and archives open properly.

➤ Test your blog on the top browsers like Chrome, Firefox, Safari and Internet Explorer and see if everything looks right.

➤ Check your contact info and contact form to see that it works well. Test your blog comment form and make sure people can easily leave comments.

➤ Test your social sharing buttons, so that people can share your posts on the top social networks.

➤ Give your visitors more ways to connect with you and subscribe to your blog as well as an option to subscribe by email.

➤ Set up Google Analytics to track your visitors, from where they come and top content pages on your website.

Your promotion goals

As you start on blogging, you will have three main goals for promoting your blog.

1.   Firstly, you need to get the word out about your new blog so that people interested in your niche can find your blog, consume your content, and spread the word.

2.   Secondly, focus on attractive an authority and gaining trust from your readers and from other influencers within your niche. Build a good relationship with top bloggers in complementary topic areas and strive to enhance your name and credibility.

3. Thirdly, engage with your niche market happens every time anyone mentions your blog. When people start discussing your content, make sure to join the discussion wherever it may be, including on your blog, social networks, forums, etc.

Remember these goals in everything you do while promoting your blog. Your goals are to get more exposure for the blog, establish yourself as an authority, and engage with your niche audience.

Ways to promote your blog

Let's learn the ways you can promote your blog as a whole. These are very important steps when you are just starting out.

Let others know about your new blog.

Try to inform everyone who encounters you should know that you have a blog. Some good ways to ensure this include the following.

>Add your blog URL to your email signature so that your email contacts can check it out. WiseStamp is a great app for anyone using Gmail or other browser-based email systems. It will even drag in your latest blog post into your signature.

>Add your blog URL to the social network you use the most, including Twitter, Facebook, LinkedIn, Google+ and Pinterest. Thus, whenever people

find you on social media, they can discover your blog as well.

➢ Add your blog URL to forum groups and signatures where you participate in discussions, preferably related to your new blog's niche.

➢ Add your blog URL to author bios of every site you are already contributing to, including other blogs you own. Maybe you already have a blog about fashion and you're starting a blog about marketing.Your author bio and about page should link to your new marketing blog.

Network with others   Hour 17

You should try to attend any networking events. Ensure to have a quick elevator pitch about your blog when people ask you what you do. If you're at a blogging conference, it's highly acceptable to let people know that you founded yourdomain.com. A blog that helps people learn about your subject matter. Even if you have a day job that you need to promote, your elevator pitch is that you are a "your job title", and you also run yourdomain.com, a blog that helps people learn more about your subject matter.

Present your blog to search engines

In Chapter 3, we suggested one of the plugins called Yoast SEO. One of the features of this SEO plugin allows you to create a custom sitemap for your blog. And you can use this sitemap to submit your blog to search engines through Google Webmaster Tools (for Google) and Bing Webmaster Tools (for Bing and Yahoo).

Present your blog to directories

There are more than hundreds of directories that will list your blog for a specific yearly fee or a permanent fee. Only a handful should be considered in terms of quality. These like DMOZ (free, but tough to get into), Best of the Web Blogs ($160 for a submission). EatonWeb Blog Directory ($40 per submission)and Yahoo Directory ($300 for 7-day listing guarantee).Some of these directories offer free listings as well, but you have to wait a very, very long time to see yours added if they add it at all.

Comment on other blogs

Commenting regularly on other relevant blogs is a great way to build relationships with top bloggers within your niche. Explore the Web to find top blogs in your niche and start commenting on their newest posts. This will help you make blog hosts and their readers aware of your existence and help you establish your own authority within your selected niche.

Contribute to other blogs in your niche

It's still a great way to get exposure within your niche so long as you are submitting good quality content to quality blogs. Find blogs that have strong social shares and community engagement as judged by the higher number of comments per post and social followers. Dig up to know the blog owners and or the editors, establish a relationship with them, then approach them to see if they are accepting new contributors on their website.

There is logic here as new contributors as opposed to guest bloggers. "Contributors," tells the blog owner or editor that you are dedicated to creating high-quality content for them as opposed to just slapping something together to promote yourself.

Create a Feedburner account

A Feedburner is a service owned by Google that allows bloggers to track the number of subscribers to your RSS feed. Use it to offer your blog visitors a way to subscribe to your blog in their favorite RSS reader.

Optimize your blog for search

Frequently creating valuable content on your blog is one way to get search engines to index your content. If you want your blog and posts to rank for particular keywords, you should always strive to optimize both for search. This can be as simple as using the area provided by Yoast SEO to add a keyword optimized SEO title and Meta description to your blog's homepage, main static pages and each one of your posts. To be on safer site on Google's side, avoid overstuffing your blog with keywords. Choose one keyword phrase to optimize on each page and post. Include it in your SEO title, meta description and inside the Alt text (alternative text) of the image on the page.

Establish your mailing list

Start earlier from the beginning to build your mailing list do not wait to get a substantial amount of traffic. On your first day of launching your blog you can get few people who love it, you want those few people to be able to give you their email address so you can keep them up to date with what is happening on your blog. Afterward, you will use this list to promote your monetization strategy. Fortunately, operating a mailing list is generally not expensive in the beginning. Some services like MailChimp allow you to have up to 2,000 subscribers with up to 12,000 emails for free, while services like Aweber allow you to have up to 5000 subscribers with unlimited emails but for $19 per month.

Look at what your competitors are doing

No need for you to reinvent the wheel when it comes to promoting your blog. Just look at what your competitors are doing in terms of marketing strategy. You can use SEO back-link tools to show you the links your competitors are getting; this will shed light on their strategies for social networks, directories,guest posting opportunities and online marketing tactics.

Look for paid advertising options

You can boost your initial traffic through paid advertising. Google AdWords allows you to pay to promote your blog on Google Search engine and their display networks. Social networks like Facebook, Twitter, LinkedIn, and Stumble Upon have their own different advertising platforms to help you drive traffic to your blog and blog posts. You may also look at advertising options on other blogs in your niche that receive a lot of traffic. This will normally be in the form of banner advertisements or sponsored reviews.

Ways to promote your blog content

To promote your blog as a whole, you need to promote your blog content, for each, individual blog post. When you promote your content, the entire blog will gain more traffic, social shares, and engagement. Following are some other ways to promote your content. Submit your posts to bookmarking and voting sites similar to directories, there are thousands of social bookmarking and voting sites. And they are similar to directories, not all of them are worth-while. Your goal is to look for social bookmarking and voting sites that have engaged users. This include like Delicious. You may want to consider establishing friendships on those networks and occasionally sharing content with them. Often, they will submit your content to the networks, particularly if you do the same for them.

Try blog promotion networks

Several networks exist exclusively for the purpose of gathering people who love to help each other promote their blog posts. The example of networks includes Triberr, Social Buzz Club, and Viral Content Buzz. You can build your own blog post promotional network as your network with others in your niche. Just like everyone connects in the Facebook group or in an email list where they can share their latest posts.

Establish yourself on social media
Hour 18

Welcome to Hour 18 to become a successful blogger, we hope by this point, you should have already claimed your preferred name on each social channel. Never forget, that social media (aside from paid advertising) is a place to connect with others, be helpful to them and display your expertise and sell their products. A place where you can meet others, trade ideas and network to form alliances. And remember to treat everyone you meet with respect. Your main aim is to be of value and engage with your current or future blog readers. The social networks you should work towards building your connections upon are listed below. Each social media platform should be utilized and approached differently. Select the one (or ones) that best fit your needs and become an expert at leveraging them to help reach your goals.

1. Facebook

Facebook has over one billion active monthly users and is the number one social media network. Many of your potential readers and future customers already have an account there. One important thing to remember is that Facebook tends to be reserved for true "social" interaction. You can initiate your blog's Facebook page and start interacting with the community that is already established but you must be careful about mixing business with pleasure on this platform.

Facebook rewards the engagement with your followers; consequently, the goal is not the quantity but quality of relevant posts and updates that engage your fans, which can be measured by the number of likes, comments and shares you receive. You should find out how to use your personal Facebook page for business by reading a different article. Also, remember that Facebook is a large place to promote your posts. You can start by using their paid advertising platform as you grow your own blog audience and reach.

2. LinkedIn

LinkedIn is another leading social network for professionals. It has more than 100 million users, it's a great place to connect with other bloggers and business owners in your niche. The network has a lot to offer when it comes to your business-related information. The shortcoming to this network is that unlike Twitter, you have to know a person already (or know their email address) before you to connect with them. Social Media stated an excellent 10 Tips series can help get you going with this platform. Read their post on 10

LinkedIn Tips for Building Your Business for more information.

3. Pinterest

While it is still largely used by women, the number of men on Pinterest is increasing. With more than two million active users daily, the statistics on Pinterest are impressive. So if you are interested in the Pinterest look for the book by the authors of this book.

4. Instagram

This site will allow you to share photographs through your mobile device. It's similar to Pinterest, in that you, but can create boards that focus on specific topics. Remember how important it is to stay centered. Make sure your the image photographs are what your audience wants to see. This is not to say you shouldn't post items of general interest, but your profile should draw your desired audience and provide value to them. Instagram's Getting Started page is a big place to learn about the platform.

5. Twitter

There are almost 200 million users on Twitter. Some say it is a one-way conversation, with 140-character (maximum) messages getting fired out constantly before. Recently they are deciding to increase the character above the 140.They twitter claim that there are a lot of people talking, but not a lot of people listening.But they have managed to build a strong, engaged following to promote their content.

6. Google+

This is more than a social media platform, Google is using Google+ as a HubSpot for identifying online movers and shakers. The company Internet giant has moved business listings from Google Places to Google+.This is the one social media platform you should definitely not ignore. Mark Traphagen stays tuned in to all things concerning Google+, and make sure to Follow Mark to stay updated.

7. YouTube   Hour 19

Youtube is now owned by Google, the videos you launch on YouTube are quickly indexed on the world's largest search engine. Remember Do not forget to apply search engine optimization (SEO) strategies on your YouTube channel and launches. Most particularly by optimizing your titles and video descriptions with a target keyword phrase.It is not wise enough to host your videos on your own blog because of the time it takes to load large video files. But YouTube is an excellent solution to the problem.You can host videos there for free, gain the SEO advantage, then embed them in your own blog.

Additional social networks

There are other social media possibilities and new ones appear on a regular basis.But, one we mentioned above are the already popular channels will serve your needs well and deliver maximum promotional benefit. Certainly, your business is unique, and you should better make use of the social media avenues that best fit your own niche and style. If there is a new known channel where your audience tends to gather, you should be there with them. Whatever you do, do it optimally, so don't overextend yourself. Everything that you can do online is a reflection of your capability.

Congratulation!!!

All we have stated in Hour 19 to become the successful blogger. You can extend your vision beyond the tips listed, you can come up with more ideas, or other creative ways to promote your blog. But remember the best bet is to start small and make adjustments to your promotional strategies along the way. Always remember to focus on key fundamentals of blogging. Maintain a clean and properly functioning blog and create good and helpful content.

Philip Knoll

NOTE

.

Chapter six

How to monetize your blog   hour 20

This chapter will teach you how to prepare your blog for monetization and strategies tips for making money from your blogs.Even if the blog has small, medium, and large audiences. If one of the reasons for starting a blog was to make money online, then this is the hour you have been waiting for. For those people who work full-time jobs, earning money from your blog is a great way to generate passive income. For those who plan to dedicate their time to the monetization strategies, it's possible to use it as the regular source of income for life.

On the previous chapters, you've learned how to set up your blog, create great content and promote your blog, then get ready now to start your monetization.

How to understand monetization

First, let' understand how monetization of any blog work, and why you should get prepared to monetize your blog.

> Passive income is the way to go so you can earn money while you sleep. This isn't completely false, but it's not as simple as it sounds either. Bloggers who are well known for their passive income generation did not achieve that on their blog one day and earn piles of money in their sleep the next. Like any other income source, passive income requires a general bit of hard work, in the beginning, to set up. until, if you do it right (and we'll teach you how), you can start earning money, even while away from the computer.

> Income reports can directly show you the path to earning top revenue.

Income reports are monthly blog posts written by bloggers who make money online, by showing exactly how much they earned throughout the month and how they did it. Be on the watch for misleading income reports. Those that show you only how much a blogger makes, but not how much they spend. Many bloggers invest a lot of money on their blog every month, in order to earn revenue. But some leave that fact out in their income reports, making it look like they are earning million of free money. When you create your own monetization plan, you'll need to keep some expenses in mind. These expenses include your web hosting, email marketing software, search and social media tools, memberships and advertising.

➢ Do not monetize until after you grow an audience

This is not true. Although you can only utilize certain monetization strategies with a growing audience,you shouldn't get your readers used to an advertisement free blog, then spring into monetization mode as soon as you hit a certain number of visitors. This might surprise and put off your original readership.

As soon as possible, put some monetization strategies in place at the very beginning, you will have the chance to earn a little money from the beginning while letting your audience know exactly what they are going to get. Ultimately, you can add or subtract monetization methods as an ongoing process to test which ones earn the most revenue, but don't feel like you have to wait to start. Now that we've identified a few misconceptions about making money through blogging, let's look at how you can generate money by blogging.

Preparing to monetize 21 hour

Before starting your blog monetization, it will be better to understand one basic thing you need to do so that to ensure your current and future monetization success:

> Start to build an email list as soon as possible. We've mentioned this before, but it is absolutely essential if you want to earn money in the blogging world. The reasons are:

1. If you start to compile email addresses at the start of your blog, you will have the chance to retain your first visitors as lifelong readers. No one has to know that initially there's only one subscriber on your mailing list.

2. Before you can have monetization strategies that need email promotion, you can use your email list to drive traffic to your blog by promoting your content.

3. Your email list subscribers are yours. You should not have contact information for fans of your page or followers on your Twitter account. Your email list, alternately, is exportable. So if your email provider decides to shut down, you take your list and move it elsewhere as opposed to losing it completely.

4. Your email list subscribers usually see your email messages than social media updates. But, Facebook reach is slim, as other networks, since most people are following a numerous number of other people and businesses. Because, getting in someone's inbox means that they will at least see your name on a regular basis, regardless of whether they open their email. And when they do open that email, you have their entire attention.

5. When you start utilizing monetization ways such as email list, affiliate marketing, or selling your own products, you already developed a loyal audience that is used to receiving and consuming your emails. This is better than starting a list and selling to your subscribers right away.

Luckily enough, email marketing does not have to cost you a lot before you start generating revenue. MailChimp allows users you to have 2,000 subscribers and send six mass emails per month(a total of 12,000 emails) for free. It's a great opportunity for those who need to start a list, but don't have the money until they start earning revenue. However, that is out of the way; let's start with some specific monetization strategies for the new blogger.

Monetization strategies for new blogs

If you have a new blog or one that doesn't receive a lot of traffic, then the following are monetization strategies you can put into practice to start your revenue generation process.

1.Affiliate marketing

Affiliate marketing allows bloggers to generate income by promoting other people's products for a small commission. This is the easiest monetization method to get into at the beginning because you can apply to most programs with little to no audience. All that you need is your blog.

Here are some examples:

For instant, if you have a blog all about reviewing WordPress themes, then you can apply to affiliate programs for any WordPress theme you want to write about and promote. Any visitors to your blog would likely be interested in WordPress themes, and therefore would be likely to buy a WordPress theme after clicking on a link to it from your site.Example like affiliate programs for WordPress themes includes Studio.Or if you have a blog about Animal, then you should apply to affiliate programs for Animal books and products. Amazon Associates is an example affiliate program to join for any niche as they sell books and products related to just about everything.

Another technique is to be an affiliate for anything you have paid for and use on your blog. So, if you use a Studio Press WordPress theme, MailChimp email marketing software, Hostgator hosting or any other product with an affiliate program, be sure to create a page on your blog with resources intended at other bloggers in the niche. As your blog gradually grows in popularity, other bloggers will want to follow in your footsteps and may sign up for the same services you use for their own blog thus generating some revenue for you. To find more other affiliate programs by doing a search for paid products and services use the search term + affiliate program.

Another way you can also go to affiliate networks sites where that connect publishers like you and merchants who want publishers to promote their products.And look at the products they have available to promote Networks like Shareasale and Clickbank.

The best practices for promoting affiliate products:

> Write reviews about the product or service and include an affiliate link to your review post.Don't just repeat information found on the product or service sales page, but write about your true experience with it. People can distinguish a thorough, honest review

from one that has done purely to generate revenue.

➢ You can create a resource page on your blog of the top products and services you recommend, including an affiliate link for each, plus a link to your detail review, if applicable.

➢ You can also get banners for the top products and services you know will appeal to your audience and put them in your blog's header, sidebar and at the end of posts.Theses affiliate product banners are also great placeholders for future advertising spots you may want to sell when you start getting a substantial amount of traffic.

➢ You should email your list whenever you write a great review or a particular affiliate program because a great special going on that your subscribers would be interested in.

➢ Be well prepared to do special promotions on your blog and email list around any Black Friday and Cyber Monday, it's the hottest time to share affiliate product sales and earn some great income.

It is Important to remember that, whenever you promote an affiliate product, make sure to include a disclaimer in your review, at the top of your resource page or in your emails that you are an affiliate of the product. It is the best way to build trust with your audience and it's also required in certain countries like the US.

2. Google AdSense

Once you have created a certain amount of content for your blog, let's say 15 to 20 blog posts, you can apply for Google AdSense. Google giant provided Google AdSense that allows publishers to generate income from advertisers who want to place ads on their Network. Once you sign up and get approved, you will be able to modify ad slots for links, banners, images, and video, and place the Google AdSense code for each of these ad slots onto your website. After an hour, Google will begin to match the best ads to your website.

The key to success of Google AdSense is to follow their guidelines and know where to place your ads for the best results. You can find out with ad placement in your blog's sidebar, below the title of individual blog posts, in your blog's header and other areas. Google even offers some good example site layouts that will help you get the most clicks for your ads.

One important thing to keep in mind about Google AdSense: If you are generating good money through affiliate marketing or selling your own products and services, the last thing to do is to encourage someone to leave your website by clicking on an ad. Once you start making good money through other monetization strategies, you may want to consider removing Google AdSense.

Monetization for blogs with a few audiences 22 hour

The moment you start building a loyal readership and a good flow of traffic, you can start looking into additional monetization strategies such as the following.

➢ Selling Ads

Depending on your niche selection, you can usually start selling ad space directly to advertisers once you get a certain traffic volume. You can manually manage ads on your blog or use platforms such as BuySellAds that can help you sell and manage ads through their platform. It's a simple process; you just place a snippet of code on your website where you want particular ad sizes and types to be displayed. It's also a great platform to use in researching your traffic volume versus how you can charge for ads.

Selling Ads sample:

1. An automobile site with 30,000 monthly impressions charges $50 per month for their 728x90-leaderboard ad space.

2. A site about culture with 35,000 monthly impressions charged $3 per 1,000 impressions per month for their 300x250 top sidebar ad space.

3. While site an investing site with 50,000 monthly impressions charged $8.75 per 1,000 impressions per month for their 728x90 leaderboard ad space.

This is a good monetization strategy that has the potential to generate continually increasing amounts of revenue based on your ability to drive more traffic to your blog. Make sure to create an advertising page on your blog and update your metrics (traffic, social audience, email list subscribers, etc)

➢ Sponsored reviews

In addition to selling ad space on your blog, you can also offer sponsored reviews.

This is where people pay you to write about their product or service on your blog. If you prefer only the products your audience will most likely be interested in, you can earn money while creating an excellent content, a win-win situation. If you choose any product because people are paying you, however, you could lose your hard earned audience as they will not be interested in the content.

When you engage in sponsored reviews, you should always remember Google guidelines about using the rel=no follow attribute for paid links, or links within a paid review.People may likely offer you more to have a dofollow link - .But use your own discretion as to whether the price advertisers offer for a sponsored review is worth risking the wrath of Google.

In order to write an excellent sponsored review, insist that you want to use the product or service for a trial period really get some insight into it. That way, you can write an honest, compelling review.

➢Selling your own products or services

If you have a few loyal following, then you don't need a large audience to start selling products or services. All you need is to be able to answer the following questions.

The first question will help you determine if there's a paying market for a product or service you can provide. The second question will help you determine what that product or service is.

Do people ask me for advice or help?

What do people ask me for advice or help for?

Here are a few quick examples:

People regularly ask you how you customized your WordPress theme's functionality or design, and want you to do the same for their blog. You can take this as a sign that you need to create an information product (such as a video tutorial series) on ways to customize WordPress themes or offer a service where you will customize WordPress themes.

People flood you with requests for prints of your photography. This is an opportunity to open an online store to sell your photography.

People regularly ask you to write content for their business. You can take this as a sign that you need to offer freelance writing/copywriting services.

People want to know how you market your blog and want to "pick your brain" about it on a quick phone call. This as a sign that you need to offer consulting services.

If you pay attention to what people ask you for most often, you'll likely discover a great product or service you can offer. Because,for one person who asks you about something, there are probably a dozen others who would ask the same thing.

Monetization for blogs with large audiences 23 hour

This is a monetization strategy that has the potential to generate continually increasing amounts of revenue based on your ability to drive more traffic to your blog. Be sure to create an advertising page on your blog and update your metrics (traffic, social audience, email list subscribers, etc.) regularly so you can increase your ad pricing on a monthly basis.

➢ Syndicating content

You've likely seen those blocks of links on sites like CNN, Time magazine and other media outlets that say "Around the Web" or "You Might Also Enjoy." These are generally created by code from content syndication networks (Outbrain, Taboola, etc.), many of which want you to have a large base of traffic before you are considered to apply as a publisher to their networks.

By including blocks of related content like this on your blog, you'll be earning revenue each time someone clicks on an article that looks interesting to them. It's a good situation for both the publisher and the reader—the publisher (you, the blogger) gets money for sharing related, valuable links. The reader gets the opportunity to explore new content and will likely think of your blog as a great source of content to check out.

➢ Selling your blog

This may be the last thing on your mind at this point, but if you have a blog that isn't directly tied to your own name, products or services, and mostly depends on ad revenue, you may want to consider selling your blog later down the road. Some blogs—like the 20 listed in this article— have earned over $1 million dollars, thanks to how much traffic received, the quality of content they house and the advertising dollars they rake in on a monthly basis. The more traffic, quality content and advertising dollars you earn with your blog, the more you can sell it for if you so choose.

Conclusion 24 hour

Thank you again for downloading this book!

I hope you've enjoyed this book and we hope that you are going to create a successful blog. From the setup level of a beginner to monetization. The next step is to consistently follows the steps stated on the book and your success is guarantee.

Finally, if you enjoyed this book, please take the time to share your thoughts and post a review on Amazon. It'd be greatly appreciated!

Thank you and good luck

Bonus: Subscribe for free videos and Audio tutorial training;

P.S. AS a token of my appreciation, I have included a free gift for you no catch, no charge. Simply click www.itechcrown.com

ABOUT THE AUTHOR

Philip Knoll is CEO of itechcrown.com , the publishing company that published several IT books. He worked at Interoute, Europe's largest voice and data network provider. Before Interoute, he was working as a senior network engineer for Globtel Internet, a significant Internet and Telephony Services Provider to the market. He has been working with Linux for more than 10 years putting a strong accent on security for protecting vital data from hackers and ensuring good quality services for internet customers. Moving to VoIP services he had to focus even more on security as sensitive billing data is most often stored on servers with public IP addresses.He has been studying QoS implementations on Linux to build different types of services for IP customers and also to deliver good quality for them and for VoIP over the public Internet. Philip has also been programming educational software's with Perl,

PHP, and Smarty for over 7 years mostly developing in-house management interfaces for IP and VoIP services.